Ultimate Music Theory
LEVEL 8 Supplemental Exams

Table of Contents

Ultimate Music Theory: *The Way to Score Success!*

The 2016 RCM Theory Syllabus **additional concepts** to the Level 8 (formerly Advanced Rudiments) Examination Requirements covered in the **UMT Supplemental LEVEL 8 Workbook** include:

♫ **Chords and Harmony**: Functional Chord Symbols and Root/Quality Chord Symbols for all Chords and Triads (in Root Position and inversions).
Identification and writing of Authentic, Half and Plagal Cadences on a Grand Staff in Keyboard Style and in Chorale Style.
Identification of Cluster Chords, Quartal Chords and Polychords.

♫ **Melody and Composition**: Melodic Passing Tones and Neighbor Tones (unaccented only) within a harmonic context of I, IV and V Chords (Major) and i, iv and V Chords (minor).
Composition of a Contrasting Period in a Major or minor key, given the first 2 measures.

♫ **Form and Analysis**: Identification of concepts from this and previous levels (in the 2016 Theory Syllabus) within short musical examples.
Application of Functional Chord Symbols (I, i, IV, iv, V, V7) and Root/Quality Chord Symbols (for example, C, Am, G7) for the implied harmonies of a melody using root position & inversions, maintaining a clearly defined harmonic rhythm.
Identification of Types of Motion: Parallel, Similar, Contrary, Oblique and Static.

♫ **Musical Terms and Signs**: New Terms and Signs have been added.

♫ **Music History**: Expanding Musical Horizons: Ordo Virtutum (Hildegard von Bingen); Sumer Is Icumen In, "Reading Rota" (Anonymous); El grillo (Josquin des Prez); "Kaboran (Gamelan Prawa)"; "Evening Raga: Bhopali".

Study and Memorize the UMT Map - LEVEL 8

Circle of Fifths

♭ B E A D G C F   ♯ F C G D A E B

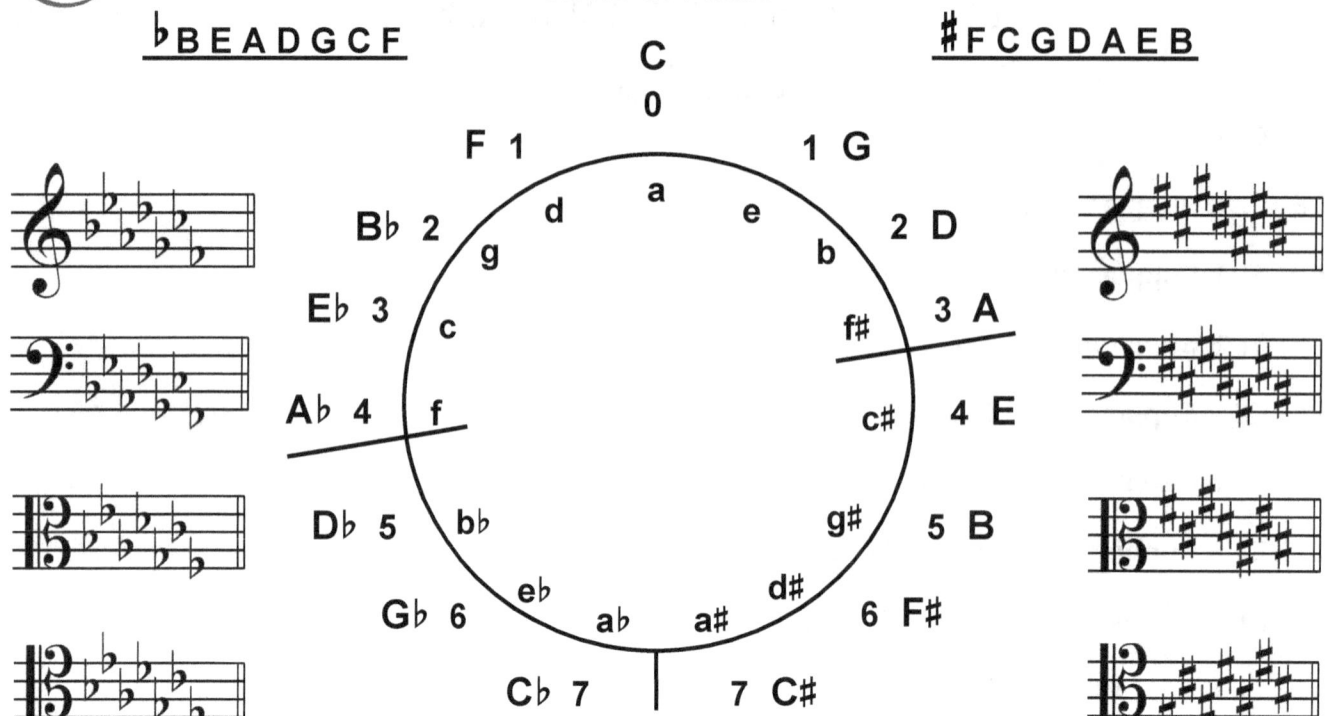

Chorale Vocal Range:

Soprano: Alto: Tenor: Bass:

Scores:

Modern Vocal: String Quartet:

Soprano   Violin I

Alto   Violin II

Tenor   Viola

Bass   Cello

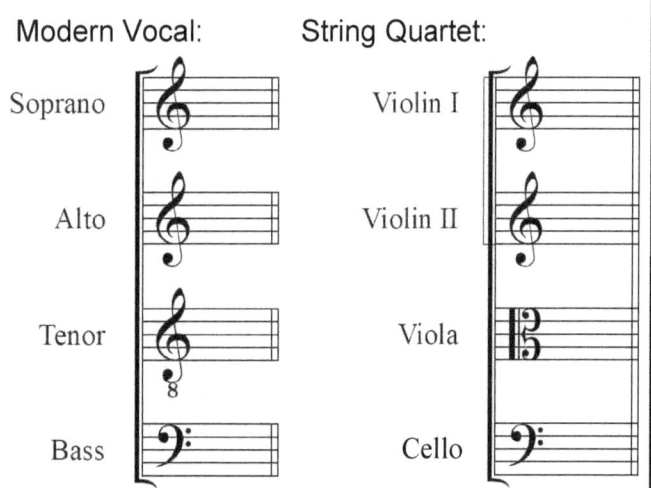

Cadences

	Major	minor
Authentic: (Perfect)	V - I, V7 - I	V - i, V7 - i
Plagal:	IV - I	iv - i
Half: (Imperfect)	I - V or IV - V*	i - V or iv - V*

(*no common note, voices descend)

Melody Writing

Parallel Period: a + a1

Contrary Period: a + b

Scale Degrees

Stable: $\hat{1}$ and $\hat{3}$

Unstable: $\hat{7}$ and $\hat{2}$

V7 - I Cadence

Complete V7 to Incomplete I (i)

or

Incomplete V7 to Complete I (i)

Tritone Tendency Tones

$\hat{7}$ to $\hat{1}$ and $\hat{4}$ to $\hat{3}$

Exam Tip: Copy the UMT Map for LEVEL 8 below. Using a blank piece of paper, write out the UMT Map from memory before beginning each practice exam and the final exam.

Circle of Fifths

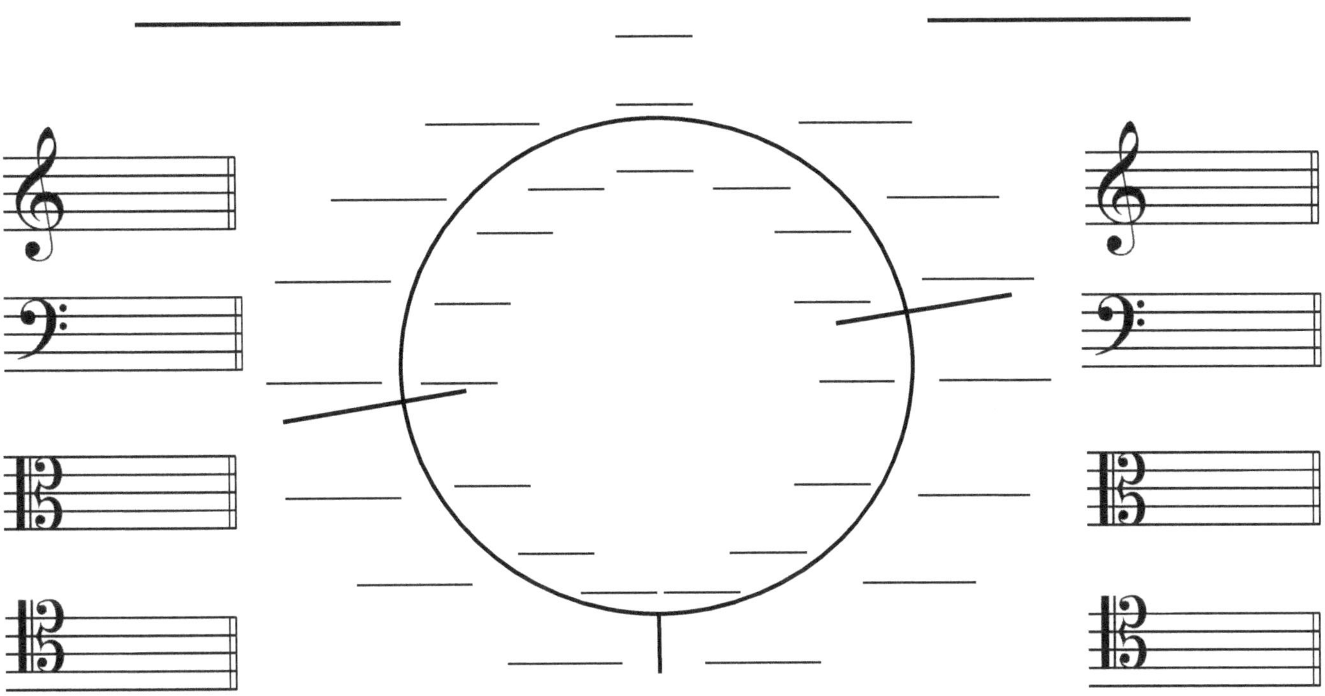

Chorale Vocal Range:

_____ : _____ : _____ : _____

Scores:

_____ Vocal: _____ Quartet:

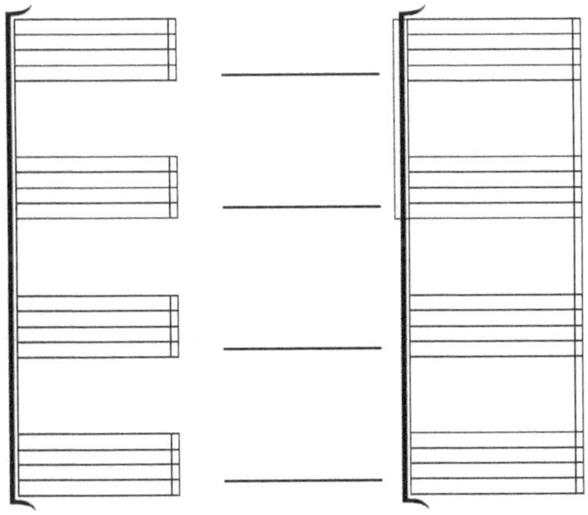

Cadences   Major   minor

Authentic: __ - __, __ - __   __ - __, __ - __
(Perfect)

Plagal: __ - __   __ - __

Half: __ - __   __ - __
(Imperfect)   or   or
                 __ - __ *   __ - __ *

(*no _____ note, voices _____)

Melody Writing   Parallel Period: ____ + ____

                     Contrary Period: ____ + ____

Scale Degrees   Stable: ____ and ____

                     Unstable: ____ and ____

V7 - I Cadence Complete __ to Incomplete __ (__)
                   or
                   Incomplete __ to Complete __ (__)

Tritone Tendency Tones   __ to __ and __ to __

Ultimate Music Theory
LEVEL 8 Supplemental Exam #1

Total Score: ____
50

Use with Advanced Exam Set #1 - Exam #1

The Ultimate Music Theory™ Advanced Rudiments Workbook, LEVELS 7 & 8 Supplemental Workbooks, Advanced Rudiments Exam Series and LEVEL 8 Supplemental Exams prepare students for successful completion of the Royal Conservatory of Music Level 8 Theory Examination.

1. a) Write the following Seventh Chords. Use accidentals. Use half notes.

Root/Quality
Chord Symbol: D7/A   E7/G♯   F°7   C♭7   B♯°7   A7/C♯

10

b) Write the following Triads in B Major. Use accidentals. Use half notes.

Functional
Chord Symbol: ii⁶   IV   vi⁶₄   iii   I⁶   vii°

2.   For each of the following Triads and Seventh Chords:

a) Name the minor key.
b) Write the Functional Chord Symbol below the staff.

10

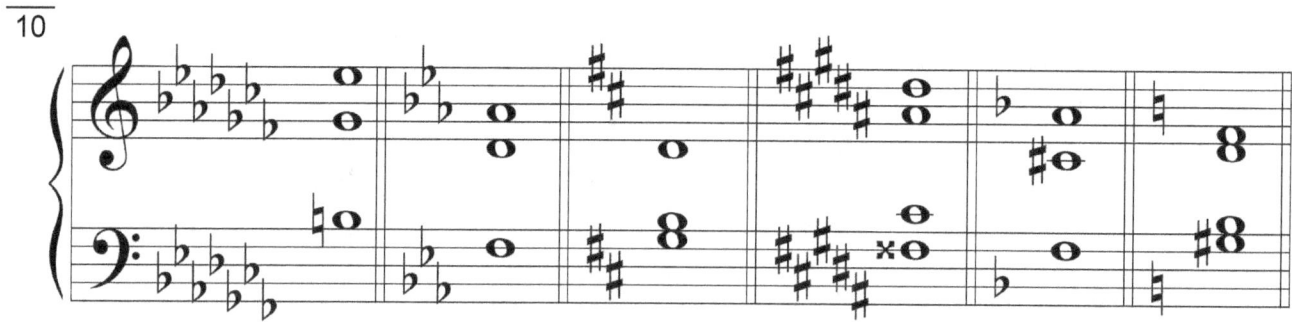

Key: a♭ minor   ____   ____   ____   ____   ____

Functional
Chord Symbol: V⁶₄   ____   ____   ____   ____   ____

3. For the following Melodic Opening:

  a) Name the key of the melody.
  b) Write the Time Signature directly on the music.
  ___
  10 c) Continue the given melody to create a Question Phrase. End on an unstable scale degree.
  d) Compose an Answer Phrase to create a Contrasting Period. End on a stable scale degree.
     (There will be more than one correct answer.)
  e) Draw a phrase mark (slur) over each phrase.
  f) Name the type of each cadence (Authentic or Half) at the end of each phrase.

Key: _____   Cadence: _____

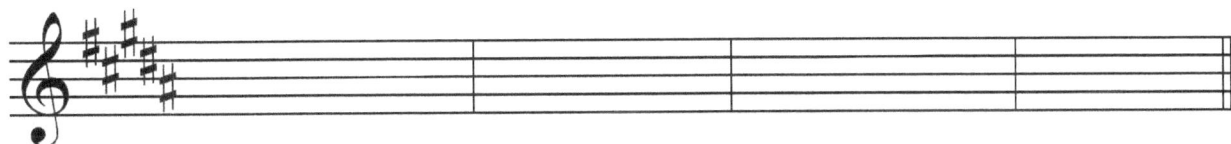

                                          Cadence: _____

4. For each of the following Cadences:

  a) Name the key.
  b) Identify the type of Cadence (Authentic, Half or Plagal) and the chords used.
  c) Identify the style as Keyboard or Chorale.
  ___
  10

Key: g minor   _____ _____ _____

Type: Plagal (iv - i) _____ _____ _____

Style: Chorale   _____ _____ _____

5. Answer any 10 (Ten) of the following.

    a) Name the Composer of "El grillo".

10 _____

    b) Name the Composer of "Ordo Virtutum".

    _____

    c) Name the Genre of "Sumer Is Icumen In".

    _____

    d) Name the Genre of "Ordo Virtutum".

    _____

    e) Name the Type of Ensemble featuring gongs, xylophones, metallophones, drums and voices.

    _____

    f) Name the plucked Indian Instrument with moveable frets and multiple strings.

    _____

    g) Name an expressive device used in "El grillo" to depict the text.

    _____

    h) Name the Texture of "Sumer Is Icumen In".

    _____

    i) Name the Texture of "Ordo Virtutum".

    _____

    j) Name the Period or Era when "El grillo" was written.

    _____

    k) Name the Period or Era when "Sumer Is Icumen In" was written.

    _____

    l) Name the Period or Era when "Ordo Virtutum" was written.

    _____

1. Add the correct Time Signature below the bracket for each of the following rhythms.

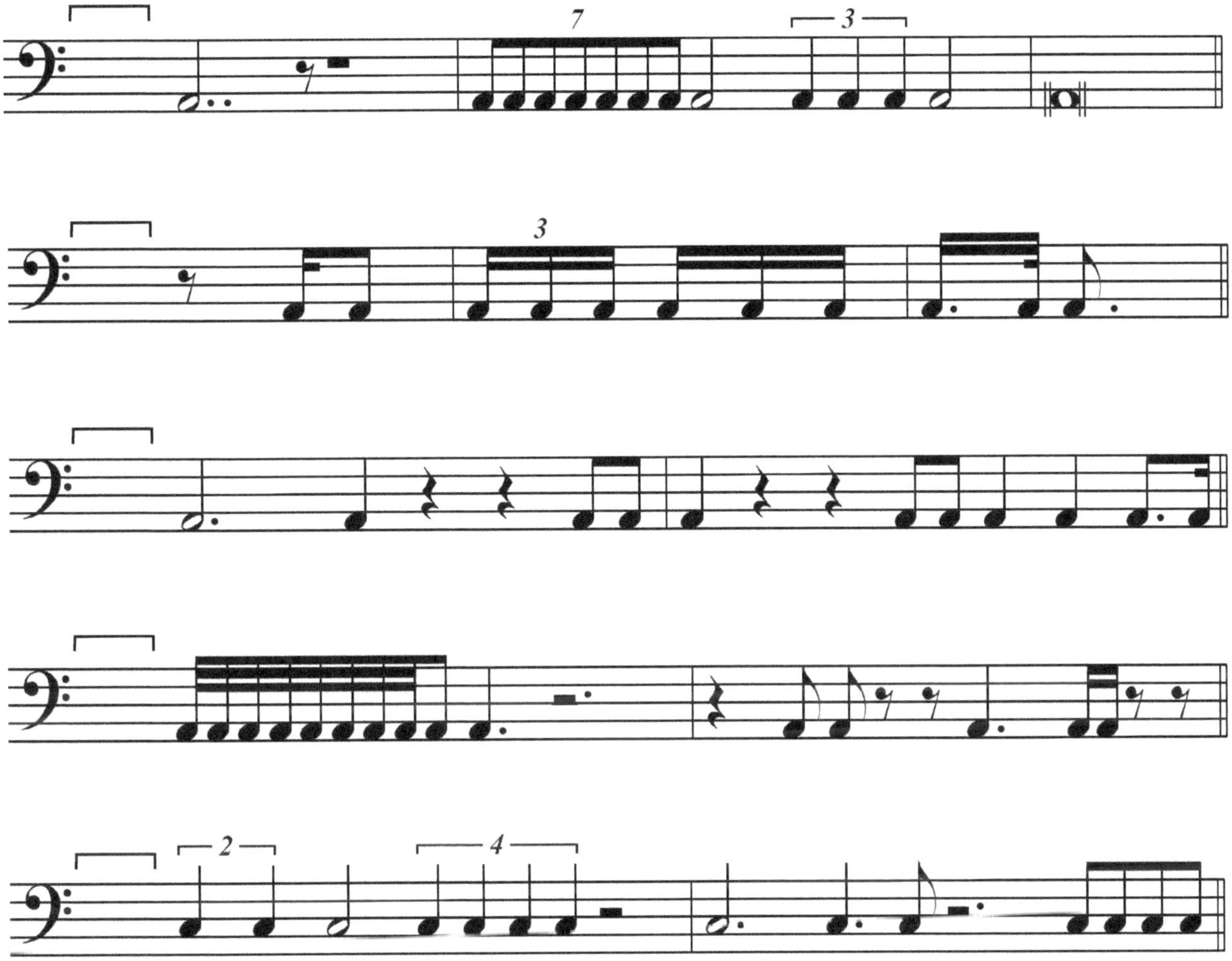

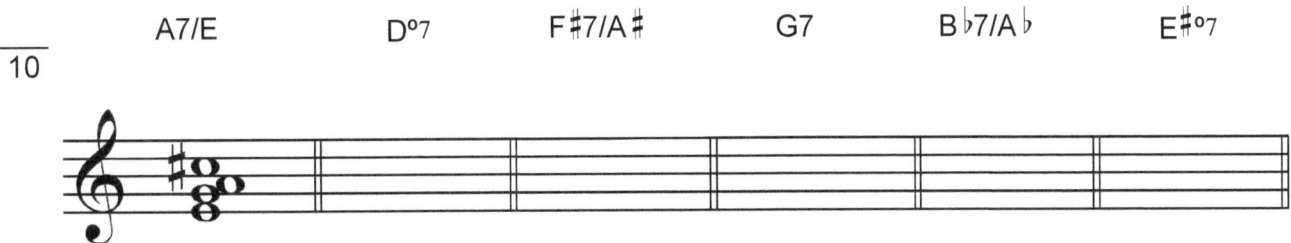

2. Write the following Seventh Chords. Use whole notes. Use accidentals.

	A7/E	D°7	F♯7/A♯	G7	B♭7/A♭	E♯°7

3. a) For each of the following triads:
   i. Name the minor key.
   ii. Write the Functional Chord Symbol below the staff.

Key: f♯ minor   _____   _____   _____   _____   _____

Functional
Chord Symbol: ii°^{6} _____   _____   _____   _____   _____

(or ii°$^6_3$)

b) For each of the following triads:
   i. Name the Major key.
   ii. Write the Root/Quality Chord Symbol above the staff.

Root/Quality
Chord Symbol: G♯°/B   _____   _____   _____   _____   _____

(or G♯dim/B)

Key: A Major   _____   _____   _____   _____   _____

4. a) Name the key of the following melody.
    b) In the given melody, write the Functional Chord Symbols on the lines below each measure.
    c) In the given melody, circle any Passing Tones. Label them as "pt".
    d) In the given melody, circle any Neighbor Tones. Label them as "nt".
    e) Rewrite the melody at the same pitch. Use a Key Signature and any necessary accidentals.

Key: _____

5. Match each musical term or sign with the English definition. (Not all definitions will be used.)

Term		Definition
tranquillo	c	a) two octaves higher
con sordino	____	b) fast
tutti	____	c̶) quiet, tranquil
grandioso	____	d) becoming faster, pressing
mit Ausdruck	____	e) with mute
quindicesima alta	____	f) grandly
stringendo	____	g) moderately, moderate
attaca	____	h) a passage for the ensemble
langsam	____	i) at the same tempo
schnell	____	j) slowly, slow
massig, mässig, mäßig (Any version may be used)	____	k) proceed without a break
		l) with expression

1. For the following Melodic Opening:

    a) Name the key of the melody.
    ___ b) Write the Time Signature below the bracket.
    10 c) Complete the first phrase. End on an unstable scale degree. Name the type of cadence.
        (There will be more than one correct answer.)
    d) Compose an Answer Phrase to create a Contrary Period. End on a stable scale degree.
        Name the type of cadence. (There will be more than one correct answer.)
    e) Draw a phrase mark (slur) over each phrase.

Key: _____   Cadence: _____

                                                    Cadence: _____

2. Write the following Close Position Solid (Blocked) Triads and Chords. Use whole notes.
    Use a Key Signature and any necessary accidentals. Write the Root/Quality Chord Symbol
    above and the Functional Chord Symbol below.

    ___
    10 a) The Submediant Triad of a minor harmonic, in first inversion.
    b) The Dominant Seventh Chord of C Major, in third inversion.
    c) The Mediant Triad of g minor harmonic, in second inversion.
    d) The Diminished Seventh Chord of c sharp minor harmonic, in root position.
    e) The Supertonic Triad of D flat Major, in root position.

Root/Quality
Chord Symbol: a) _____ b) _____ c) _____ d) _____ e) _____

Functional
Chord Symbol: a) _____ b) _____ c) _____ d) _____ e) _____

3. Add Bar Lines to complete the following rhythms.

10

4. Write the term or word for each statement. Use the following terms or words. (Not all terms or words will be used.)

Morality Play   Plainchant   Ordo Virtutum   Canon   Word Painting   Drone

10   Tala   Sitar   Stringendo   Allargando   Renaissance   Raga   Medieval

a) _____ - The technique of writing music that used melody, rhythm and/or harmony to reflect the meaning of the text.

b) _____ - A Medieval liturgical drama composed around the year 1151 by Hildegard of Bingen.

c) _____ - A multi-stringed instrument with moveable frets, a hollow neck and a gourd-shaped resonance chamber.

d) _____ - The genre of a medieval drama and music that used allegorical or symbolic figures to teach a religious idea.

e) _____ - Meaning "color, passion or emotion", the melodic structure is based on a pattern of pitches and intervals.

f) _____ - Meaning "clap", a musical meter that repeats in a rhythmic cycle from the beginning to the end of the music.

g) _____ - A simple round sung by 2 or more voices where, when each voice finished, it starts again at the beginning.

h) _____ - A modal melody in free rhythm, with a monophonic texture, used with Latin texts in the liturgies.

i) _____ - A tempo mark that indicates pressing, to press ahead, becoming faster.

j) _____ - A tempo mark that indicates to become slower, broadening.

5.   This excerpt is taken from Ultimate Music Theory Student Olivia Allen's composition entitled "Sonatina in C Major". Analyze this excerpt by answering the questions below.

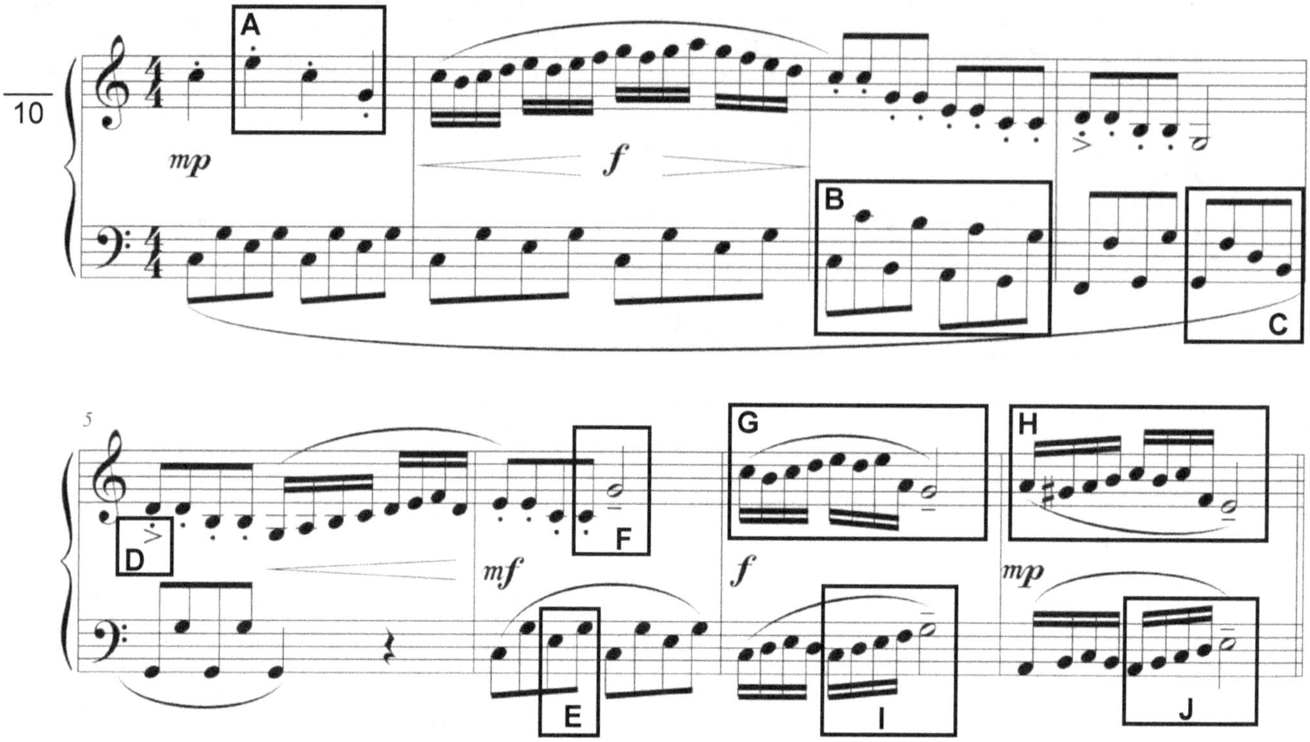

a) For the triad at **A**, identify: Root: _____;   Quality: _____;   Position: _____.

b) Identify the intervals at **B** as an example of: ☐ Parallel Fifths or   ☐ Parallel Eighths

c) For the chord at **C**, identify: Root: _____;   Quality: _____;   Position: _____.

d) Name the signs at **D**: _____

e) Identify the interval at **E**: _____.   Identify the interval at **F**: _____.

f) Identify the relationship of the notes at **G** and **H** as: ☐ Transposition or ☐ Inversion.

g) For the Pentascale at **I**, identify: Root: _____;   Quality: _____.

h) For the Pentascale at **J**, identify: Root: _____;   Quality: _____.

i) In this excerpt, identify the number of Tenuto Marks (Tenuto Signs): _____.

j) In this excerpt, identify the number of Slurs (Phrases): _____;   Ties: _____.

1. For each of the following melodic examples:

   i)   Name the Key Signature.
   ii) Add the Time Signature directly on the staff.
   iii) Identify the Type of Melodic Motion between the two voices as Parallel, Similar, Contrary, Oblique or Static.

a) Key: ___D flat Major___

   Motion: ___Similar___

b) Key: _____

   Motion: _____

c) Key: _____

   Motion: _____

d) Key: _____

   Motion: _____

e) Key: _____

   Motion: _____

f) Key: _____

   Motion: _____

2. Write the melodic interval below the given note. Use whole notes.

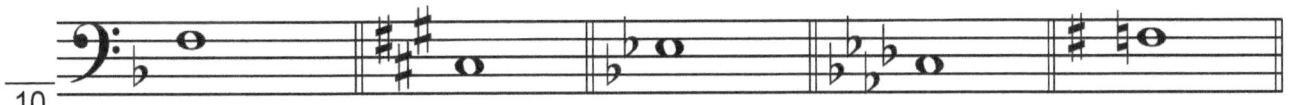

10 _____

   a) diminished 10   b) Augmented 5   c) Major 14   d) Perfect 11   e) diminished 15

3. For the following Melodic Opening:

    a) Name the key of the melody.

    b) Complete the first phrase. End on an unstable scale degree. Name the type of cadence. (There will be more than one correct answer.)

    c) Compose an Answer Phrase to create a Contrary Period. End on a stable scale degree. Name the type of cadence. (There will be more than one correct answer.)

    d) Draw a phrase mark (slur) over each phrase.

<u>10</u>

Key: _____   Cadence: _____

Cadence: _____

4. Circle TRUE or FALSE for each of the following statements.

    a) TRUE or FALSE: Hildegard von Bingen's *Ordo Virtutum* uses Polyphonic Texture.

<u>10</u> b) TRUE or FALSE: *Sumer Is Icumen In* uses Monophonic Texture.

    c) TRUE or FALSE: *El grillo* uses Word Painting to connect the text with the music.

    d) TRUE or FALSE: An *ostinato* is a melodic or rhythmic pattern that is heard only once.

    e) TRUE or FALSE: A Morality Play is a Medieval genre that combines music and drama.

    f) TRUE or FALSE: Cluster Chords combine 2 or more different chords to create dissonance.

    g) TRUE or FALSE: A Gamelan is a traditional Javanese instrumental ensemble.

    h) TRUE or FALSE: Meaning "to clap", *tala* provides rhythmic structure in Indian Music.

    i) TRUE or FALSE: Meaning "color", a *raga* is a 5-stringed plucked instrument with frets.

    j) TRUE or FALSE: A *frottola* is a secular polyphonic 15th Century Italian vocal genre.

5. Analyze this excerpt from Olivia Allen's Sonatina in C Major by answering the questions below.

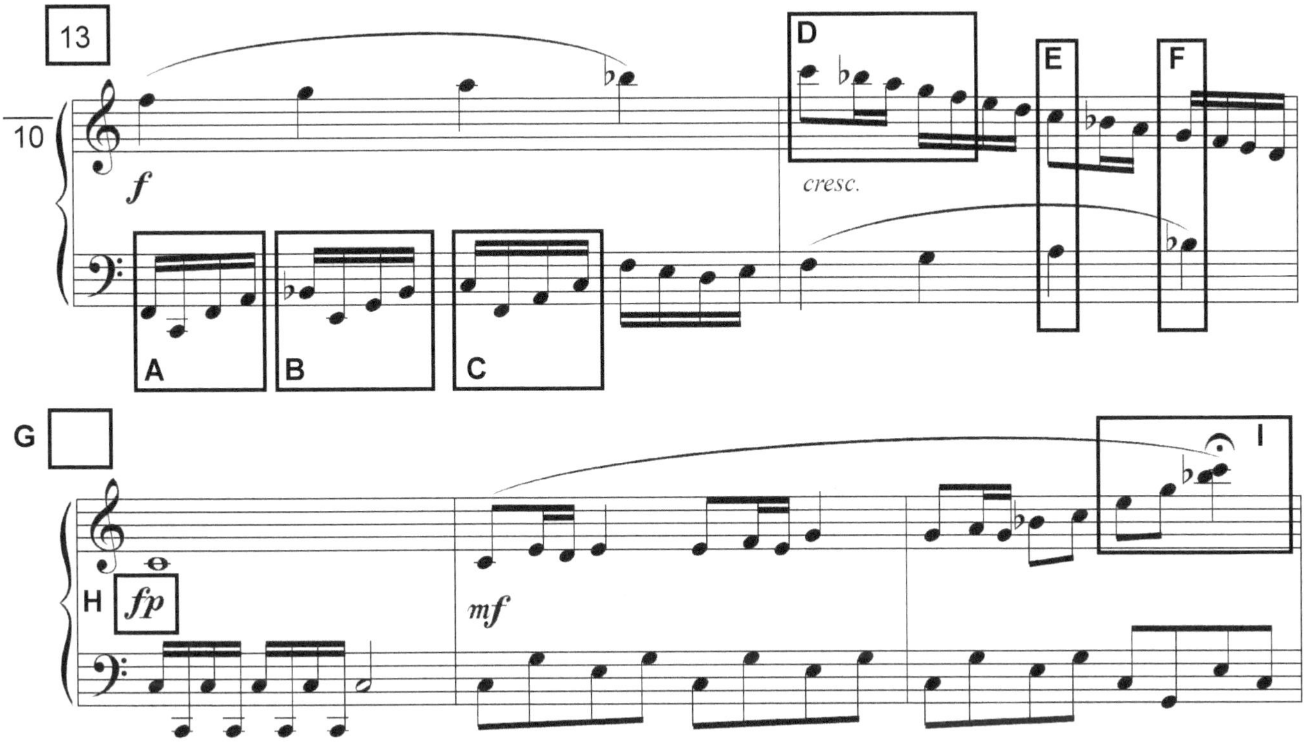

a) In this excerpt, an accidental has been added. What Key is formed as a result? _____ .

b) For the triad at **A**, identify: Root: _____ ;   Quality: _____ ;   Position: _____ .

c) For the triad at **B**, identify: Root: _____ ;   Quality: _____ ;   Position: _____ .

d) For the triad at **C**, identify: Root: _____ ;   Quality: _____ ;   Position: _____ .

e) For the Pentascale at **D**, identify: Direction: _____   Quality: _____ .

f) For the Interval at **E**, name the notes: _____ _____ .   Name the interval: _____ .

g) For the Interval at **F**, name the notes: _____ _____ .   Name the interval: _____ .

h) This excerpt begins on Measure 13. Add the correct Measure Number at **G**.

i) Explain the Dynamic Sign at **H**. _____ .

j) For the chord at **I**, identify: Type: _____ ;   Position: _____ .

Ultimate Music Theory
LEVEL 8 Supplemental Exam #5

Total Score: _____
50

Use with Advanced Exam Set #2 - Exam #1

1. a) Write the following harmonic intervals below each of the given notes.

10

Major 10   Augmented 5   diminished 8   minor 13   Perfect 4

b) Invert the above intervals in the Alto Clef. Name the inversions.

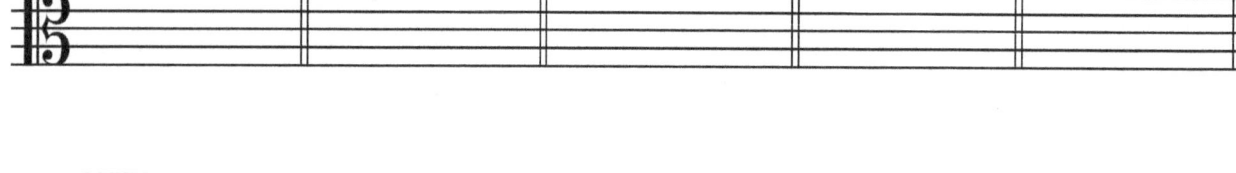

_____   _____   _____   _____   _____

2. For the following Melodic Opening:

a) Name the key of the melody.

10 b) Continue the given melodic opening to create a Question Phrase. End on an unstable scale degree. (There will be more than one correct answer.)

c) Compose an Answer Phrase to create a Contrasting Period. End on a stable scale degree. (There will be more than one correct answer.)

d) Draw a phrase mark (slur) over each phrase.

e) Name the type of each Cadence as Authentic or Half.

Key: _____   Cadence: _____

Cadence: _____

3. For each of the following triads or chords:

   a) Name the minor key.
   ___ b) Write the Root/Quality Chord Symbol above each Triad or Chord.
   10 c) Write the Functional Chord Symbol below each Triad or Chord.

Root/Quality
Chord Symbol: _____ _____ _____ _____ _____

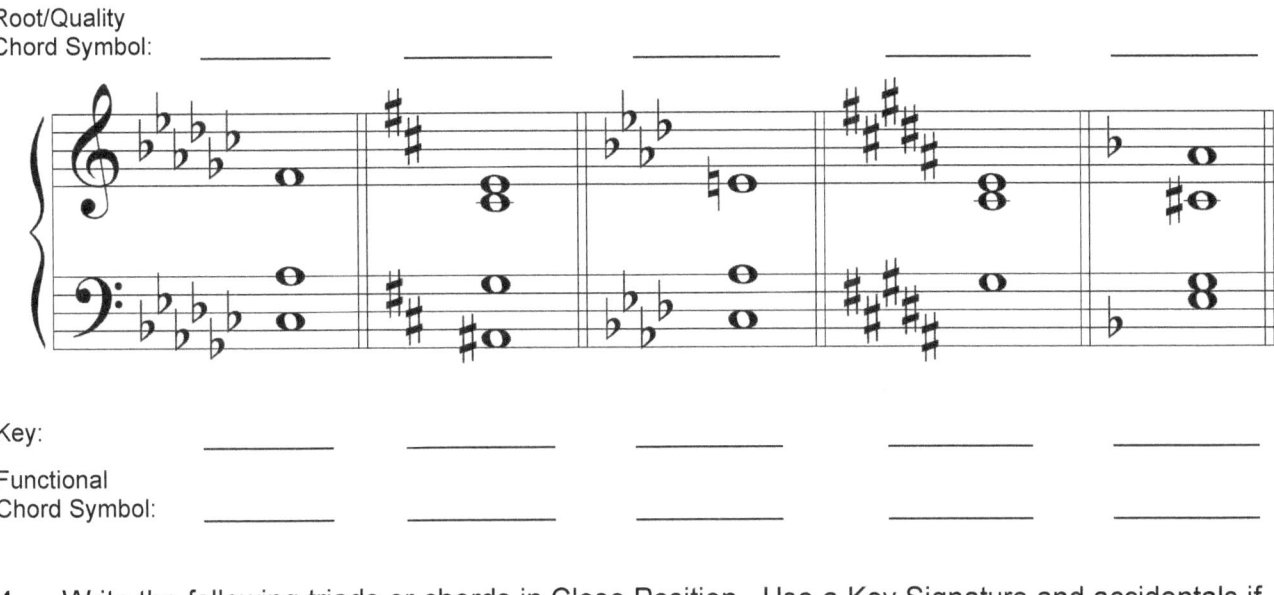

Key: _____ _____ _____ _____ _____

Functional
Chord Symbol: _____ _____ _____ _____ _____

4. Write the following triads or chords in Close Position. Use a Key Signature and accidentals if needed. Use whole notes.

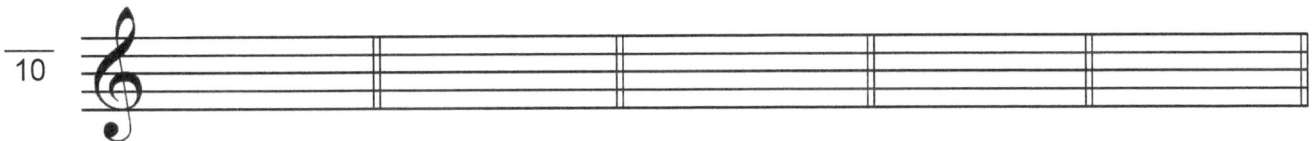

Key:	B♭ Major	C Major	a minor	f♯ minor	F Major
Functional Chord Symbol:	IV ^{6}	vii°	V $^4_2$	vii°7	I $^6_4$

Root/Quality
Chord Symbol: C♯7/E G+/B B°7 Bm/D D/A

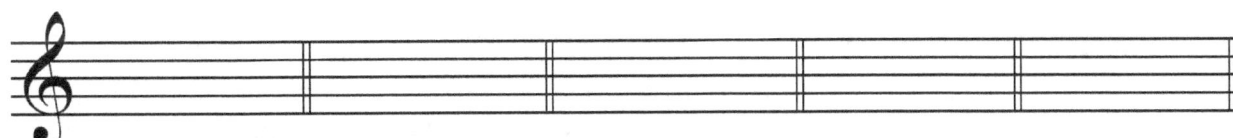

Key: F♯ Major e minor c minor G Major g minor

5. Analyze this excerpt from Olivia Allen's Sonatina in C Major by answering the questions below.

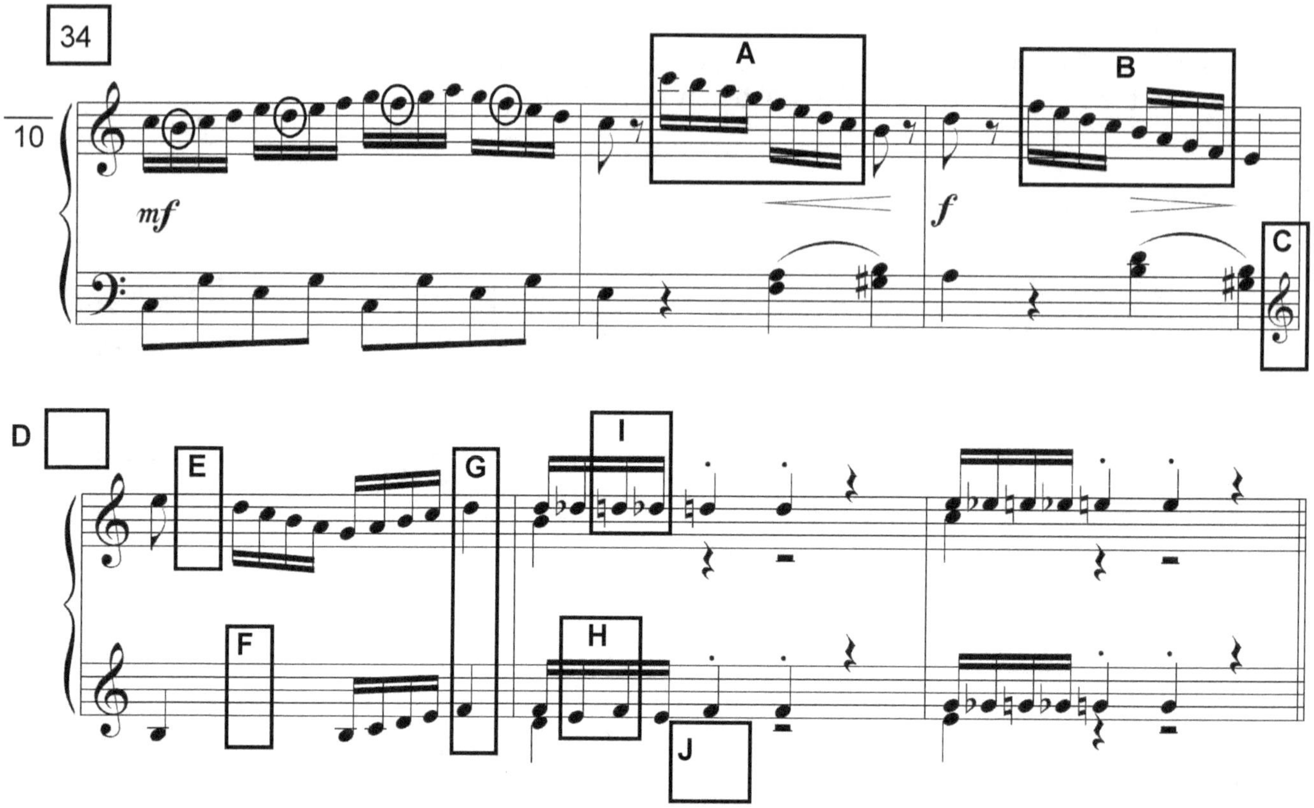

a) In M. 34, identify each circled note on the music as pt (passing tone) or nt (neighbour tone).

b) Identify the Modes at **A**: _____ ;   **B**: _____ .

c) Explain the sign at **C**. _____

d) This excerpt begins on Measure 34. Add the correct Measure Number at **D**.

e) Identify and add the correct rest at **E**: _____ ;   **F**: _____ .

f) For the Interval at **G**, name the notes: _____ _____ .   Name the interval: _____ .

g) Identify the distances as WS (whole step) or HS (half step) at **H**: _____ ;   **I**: _____ .

h) Identify the Texture in the final 2 measures as: ☐ Monophonic or ☐ Polyphonic.

i) Add the correct rest at **J**. Explain why this rest is written below the staff: _____

_____ .

1. Write the following Chords and Triads in Close Position. Use whole notes. Observe the Key Signature and use any accidentals as necessary.

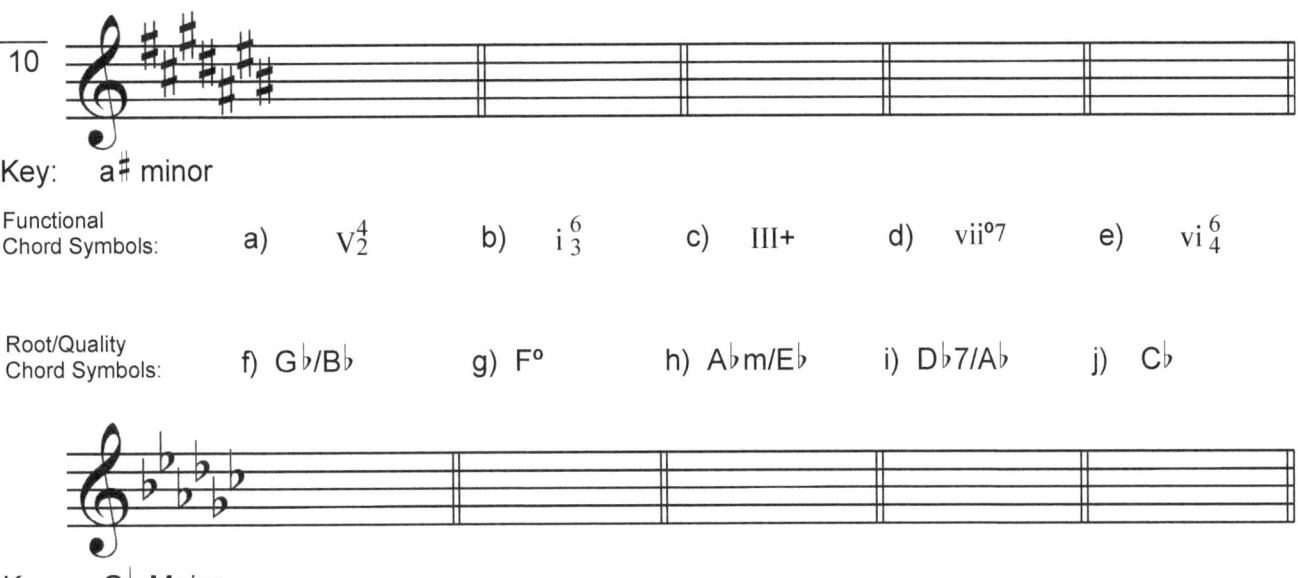

10

Key: a♯ minor

Functional
Chord Symbols: a) V_2^4 b) i_3^6 c)   III+   d)   vii°7   e)   vi$_4^6$

Root/Quality
Chord Symbols: f) G♭/B♭   g) F°   h) A♭m/E♭   i) D♭7/A♭   j) C♭

Key: G♭ Major

2. For the following Melodic Opening:

    a) Name the key of the melody.
10 b) Continue the given melodic opening to create a Question Phrase. End on an unstable scale degree. (There will be more than one correct answer.)
    c) Compose an Answer Phrase to create a Contrasting Period. End on a stable scale degree. (There will be more than one correct answer.)
    d) Draw a phrase mark (slur) over each phrase.
    e) Name the type of each Cadence as Authentic or Half.

Key: _____   Cadence: _____

Cadence: _____

3. Explain the meaning of the following terms.

    a) *comodo con espressione:* _____.

 ——
 10 b) *mesto ed ritenuto:* _____.

    c) *pizzicato:* _____.

    d) *sotto voce:* _____.

    e) *agitato e vivo:* _____.

4. Identify the work to which each of the following statements applies by writing the appropriate letter (A, B or C) in the space before each statement.

     A - Ordo Virtutum
  —— B - Sumer Is Icumen In
 10 C - El grillo

    a) _____ This work is also known as a "Reading Rota".

    b) _____ This work is written in Monophonic Texture.

    c) _____ This Genre of this work is a morality play.

    d) _____ The Genre of this work is a frottola.

    e) _____ This Genre of this work is a vocal work in the form of a round.

    f) _____ This work is based on playful poems and uses word painting.

    g) _____ This work features ostinato in the two bottom voices.

    h) _____ This work features Latin text and unmeasured rhythm.

    i) _____ The English translation of this work is "the cricket".

    j) _____ This work was written by Hildegard von Bingen.

5. Analyze this excerpt from Olivia Allen's Sonatina in C Major by answering the questions below.

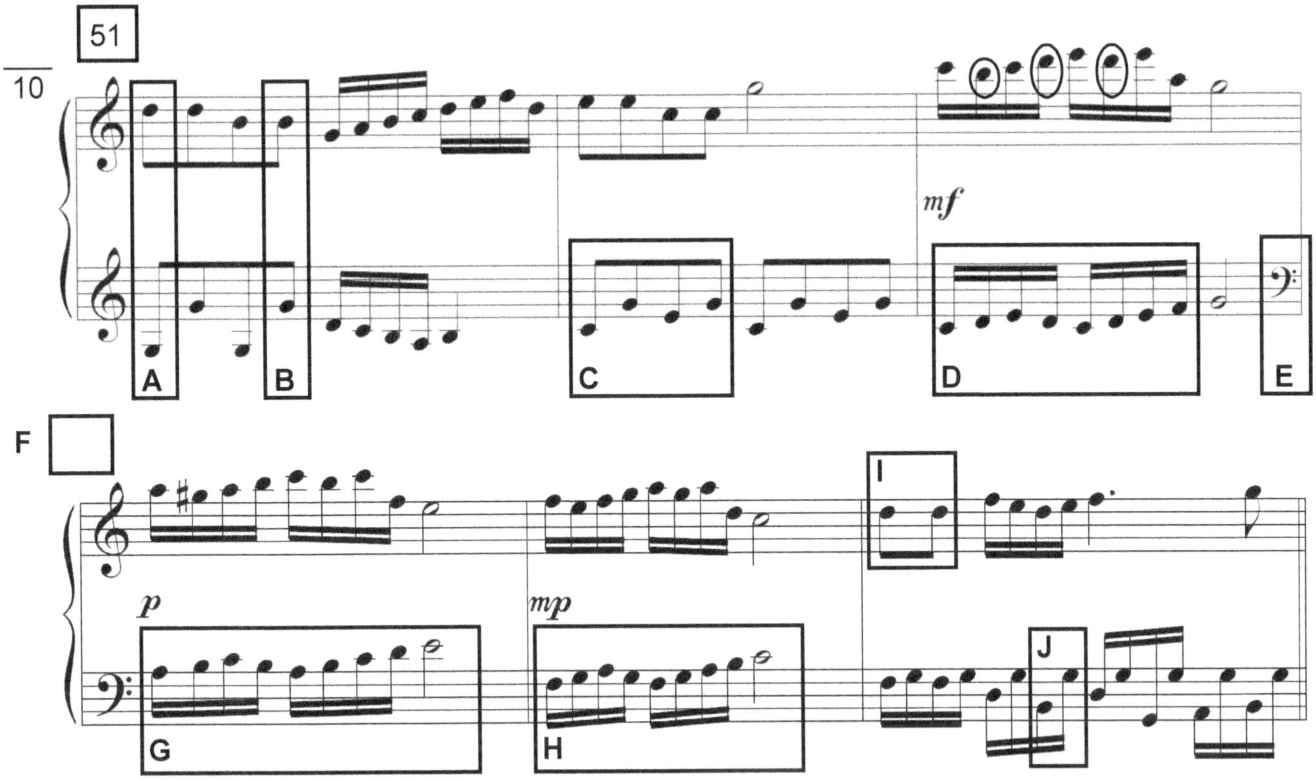

a) For the Interval at **A**, name the notes: _____ _____.   Name the interval: _____.

b) For the Interval at **B**, name the notes: _____ _____.   Name the interval: _____.

c) For the Triad at **C**, identify: Root: _____   Quality: _____   Position: _____.

d) In M. 53, identify each circled note on the music as pt (passing tone) or nt (neighbour tone).

e) Circle to identify the movement of the notes at **D** as: Conjunct   or   Disjunct.

f) Explain the sign at **E**: _____.

g) This excerpt begins on Measure 51. Add the measure number at **F**.

h) Circle the relationship of the melodic pattern at **G** and **H** as: Transposition   or   Inversion.

i) For the Interval at **I**, name the notes: _____ _____.   Name the interval: _____.

j) For the Interval at **J**, name the notes: _____ _____.   Name the interval: _____.

1. a) Write the Root/Quality Chord Symbols above the following Triads and Chords.

___
10

Root/Quality
Chord Symbols: a) _____ b) _____ c) _____ d) _____ e) _____

Key: C# Major

b) Write the Functional Chord Symbols below the following Triads and Chords.

Key: ab minor

Functional
Chord Symbols: f) _____ g) _____ h) _____ i) _____ j) _____

2. For the following Melodic Opening:

___
10

a) Name the key of the melody.

b) Continue the given melodic opening to create a Question Phrase. End on an unstable scale degree. (There will be more than one correct answer.)

c) Compose an Answer Phrase to create a Contrasting Period. End on a stable scale degree. (There will be more than one correct answer.)

d) Draw a phrase mark (slur) over each phrase.

e) Name the type of each Cadence as Authentic or Half.

Key: _____   Cadence: _____

Cadence: _____

3.   Provide an answer (the term in the correct language) for each of the following.

   a) A German Term meaning "very":   _____

$\overline{10}$ b) A French Term meaning "fast":   _____

   c) An Italian Term meaning "with mute":   _____

   d) A German Term meaning "moving":   _____

   e) A French Term meaning "slowly":   _____

   f) An Italian Term meaning "broadly":   _____

   g) A French Term meaning "yield; hold the tempo back":   _____

   h) An Italian Term meaning "the same tempo":   _____

   i) A term for a bowed string instrument that means
       "resume bowing after a *pizzicato* passage":   _____

   j) A term for a bowed string instrument that means
       "pluck the string instead of bowing":   _____

4.   a) Write the following harmonic intervals below each of the given notes.

$\overline{10}$

| Augmented 13 | diminished 5 | Major 14 | Perfect 4 | minor 9 |

   b) Invert the above intervals in the same clef. Name the inversions.

_____   _____   _____   _____   _____

5. Match each description in the left column with the correct chord in the right column.

a)

$\overline{10}$ _____ vii°7 in c♯ minor

b)

_____ Polychord

c)

_____ Submediant Triad in E Major

d)

_____ V^6_5 in E Major

e)

_____ Quartal Chord

f)

_____ V^4_3 in c♯ minor

g)

_____ Cluster Chord

h)

_____ G♯m/B

i)

_____ E+/B♯

j)

_____ Submediant Triad in c♯ minor

Ultimate Music Theory
LEVEL 8 Supplemental Exam #8
Use with Advanced Exam Set 2 - Exam #4

Total Score: _____
50

1. Provide the answer for any 10 (TEN) of the following.

    a) Name one important Renaissance Composer: _____

10 b) Name one important Medieval Composer: _____

    c) Name the texture when all voices have the same
        rhythmic pattern, creating a blocked chordal style: _____

    d) Name the texture of a single unaccompanied melody: _____

    e) Name a Renaissance Secular Polyphonic Vocal Genre: _____

    f) Name the term for music performed without
        accompaniment (literally meaning "for the chapel"): _____

    g) Name the title of one Medieval Era vocal work: _____

    h) Name the term when the music mirrors the text/words: _____

    i) Name one instrumental ensemble associated with
        "Java" ("Javanese") Music: _____

    j) Name the Medieval Genre using a monophonic modal
        melody with unmeasured rhythm and Latin text: _____

    k) Name the multi-stringed plucked instrument with
        frets that is associated with the music of India: _____

    l) Name the Medieval Genre that combined drama and
        music to teach appropriate/desirable behavior: _____

    m) Name the Contrapuntal Texture that combines 2 or
        more independent melodic lines: _____

2. In the given clef, write the following Seventh Chords. Use a Key Signature. Use half notes.

10

vii°⁷ of b♭ minor   V$^4_2$ of e minor   V$^6_5$ of E Major   V$^4_3$ of c minor   V⁷ of B♭ Major

3.   For the following Melodic Opening:

___
10

a) Name the key of the melody.
b) Write the Time Signature directly on the music.
c) Complete the given melodic opening to create a Question Phrase. End on an unstable scale degree. (There will be more than one correct answer.)
d) Compose an Answer Phrase to create a Contrasting Period. End on a stable scale degree. (There will be more than one correct answer.)
e) Draw a phrase mark (slur) over each phrase.

Key: _____

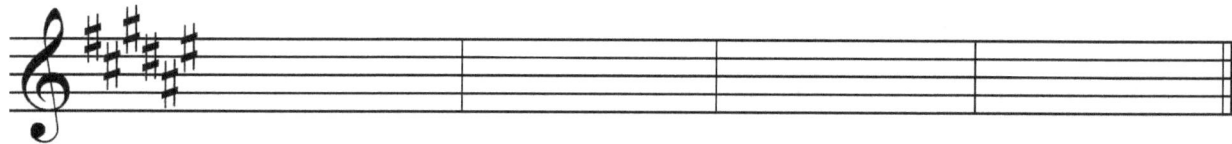

4.   Circle whether the rests in each measure are CORRECT or INCORRECT.

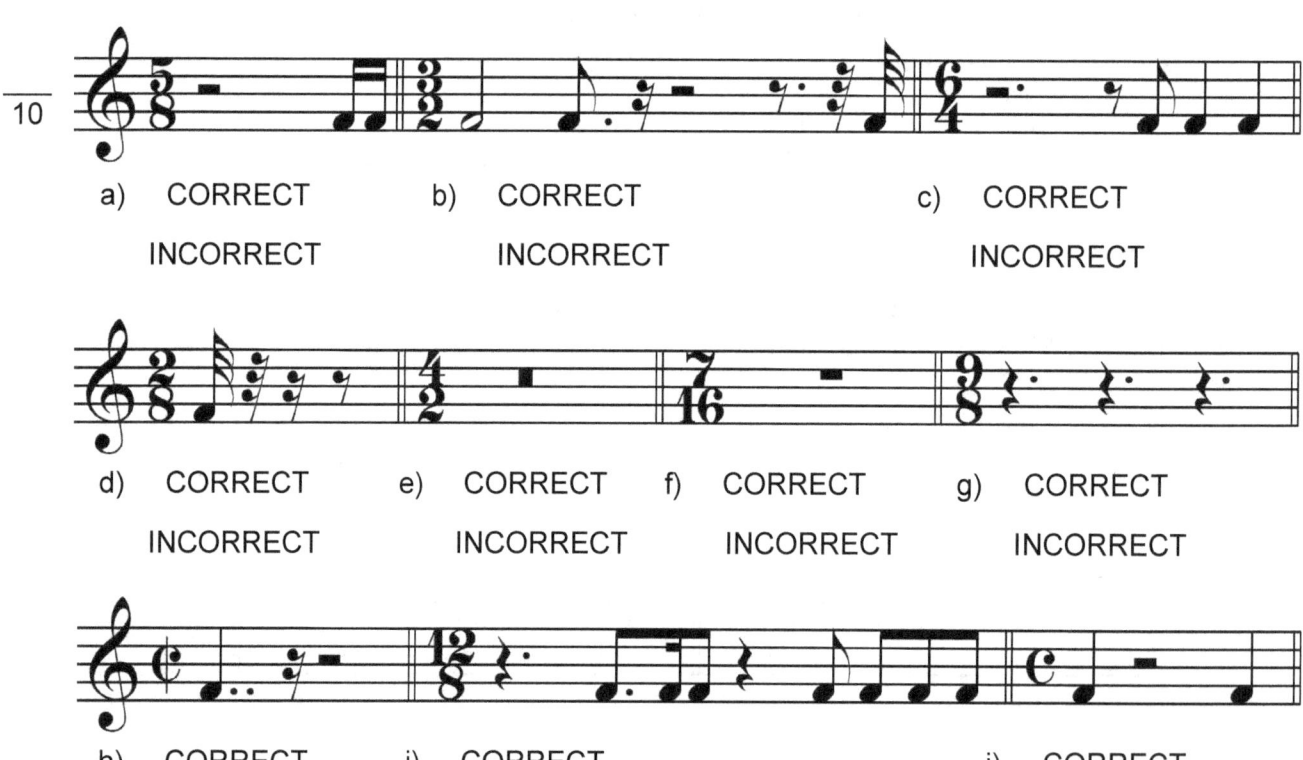

| a) | CORRECT | b) | CORRECT | | c) | CORRECT |
| | INCORRECT | | INCORRECT | | | INCORRECT |

| d) | CORRECT | e) | CORRECT | f) | CORRECT | g) | CORRECT |
| | INCORRECT | | INCORRECT | | INCORRECT | | INCORRECT |

| h) | CORRECT | i) | CORRECT | | j) | CORRECT |
| | INCORRECT | | INCORRECT | | | INCORRECT |

5.   Write the following cadences. Use a Key Signature and any necessary accidentals. Use the correct note values (observing any given rests). There will be more than one correct answer for each Cadence.

10   a) Plagal (IV - I) Cadence in E Major written in Chorale Style.
   b) Authentic (V - i) Cadence in b minor written in Keyboard Style.
   c) Half (iv - V) Cadence in d minor written in Chorale Style.

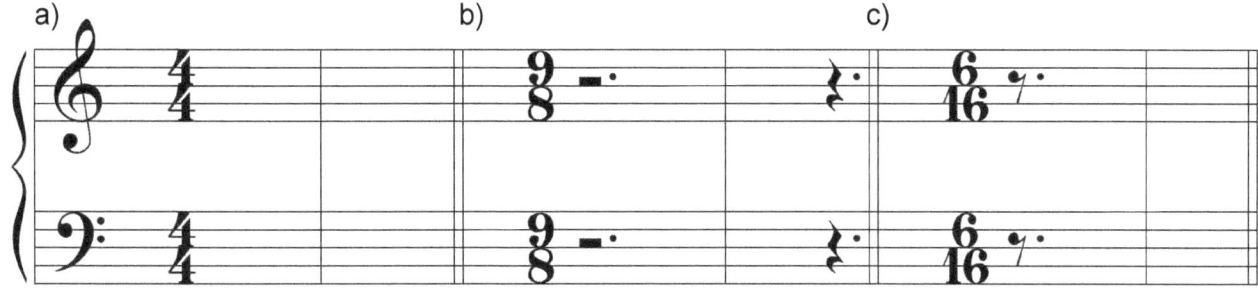

   d) Half (i - V) Cadence in f minor written in Keyboard Style.
   e) Authentic (V - I) Cadence in G Major written in Keyboard Style.
   f) Plagal (iv - i) Cadence in c minor written in Chorale Style.

   g) Plagal (IV - I) Cadence in E♭ Major written in Chorale Style.
   h) Half (I - V) Cadence F Major written in Chorale Style.
   i) Authentic (V - i) Cadence in g minor written in Keyboard Style.
   j) Half (IV - V) Cadence in D Major written in Keyboard Style.

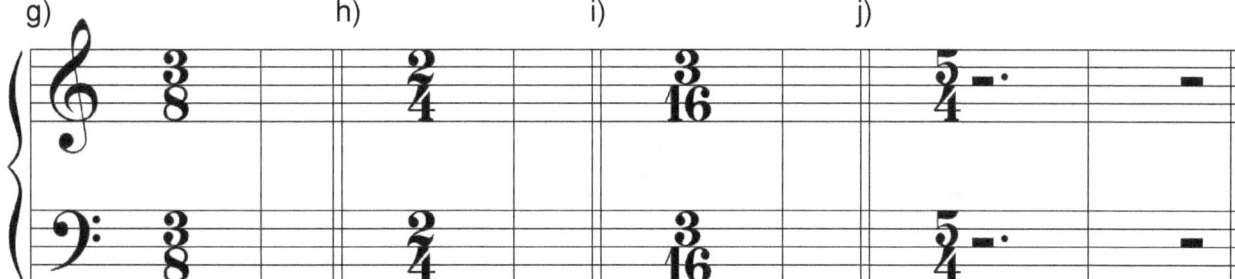

1. a) Write the following Solid (Blocked) Triads or Chords. Use a Key Signature and any necessary accidentals. Use whole notes. Write the Root/Quality Chord Symbol above and the Functional Chord Symbol below.

___
10

Dominant 7th Chord of f♯ minor, 3rd inversion.

Root/Quality
Chord Symbol: _____

Functional
Chord Symbol: _____

Diminished 7th Chord of f minor, root position.

Root/Quality
Chord Symbol: _____

Functional
Chord Symbol: _____

Subtonic Triad of g♯ minor, 2nd inversion.

Root/Quality
Chord Symbol: _____

Functional
Chord Symbol: _____

Mediant Triad of D♭ Major, 1st inversion.

Root/Quality
Chord Symbol: _____

Functional
Chord Symbol: _____

Submediant Triad of c♯ minor, 2nd inversion.

Root/Quality
Chord Symbol: _____

Functional
Chord Symbol: _____

Leading Note Triad of B Major, 1st inversion.

Root/Quality
Chord Symbol: _____

Functional
Chord Symbol: _____

b) For each of the following Dominant Seventh Chords, name the Key. Write the Root/Quality Chord Symbol above and the Functional Chord Symbol below.

Root/Quality
Chord Symbol: _____   _____   _____   _____

Key: _____   _____   _____   _____

Functional
Chord Symbol: _____   _____   _____   _____

2.   a) For each of the following Cadences:
    i) Name the key.
    ii) Name the type of cadence (Authentic, Plagal or Half).

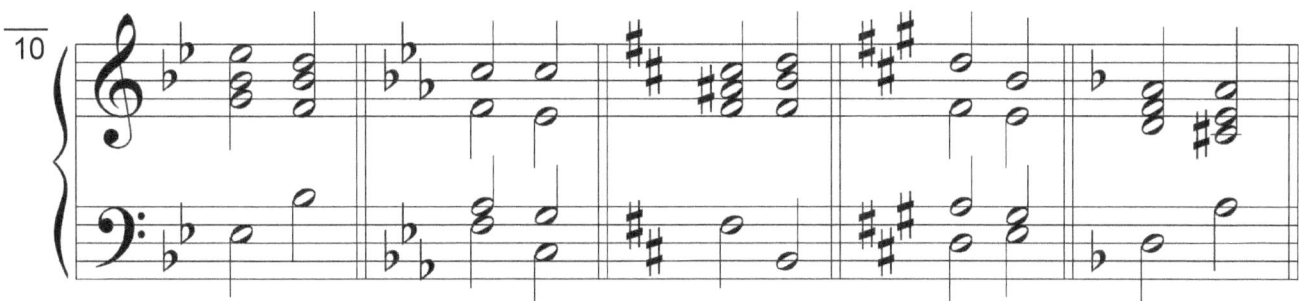

Key: _____ _____ _____ _____ _____

Cadence: _____ _____ _____ _____ _____

    b) For each of the following melodies:
    iii) Name the key.
    iv) Write a cadence in Keyboard Style below the bracketed notes.
    v) Label the chords using Functional Chord Symbols.
    vi) Name the type of cadence as Authentic, Half or Plagal.

Key: _____ _____ _____

Cadence: _____

Key: _____ _____ _____

Cadence: _____

3. a) Write the scale, ascending and descending. Use accidentals. Use whole notes.
    Identify the name of the Mode (the Modal Scale) for each of the scales.

    i) E flat Major Scale, from Subdominant to Subdominant. Mode: _____.

    __10

    ii) F sharp Major Scale, from Supertonic to Supertonic. Mode: _____.

    iii) B flat Major Scale, from Dominant to Dominant. Mode: _____.

    b) Write the minor Pentatonic Scale starting on F. Use any standard version. Use whole notes.

    c) Write the Octatonic Scale starting on F. Use any standard version. Use whole notes.

    d) Write the Blues Scale starting on F. Use any standard version. Use whole notes.

    e) Write the Whole-Tone Scale starting on F. Use any standard version. Use whole notes.

4. a) Add rests below the brackets to complete each of the following measures.

b) Add the correct Time Signature below each bracket to complete the following rhythms.

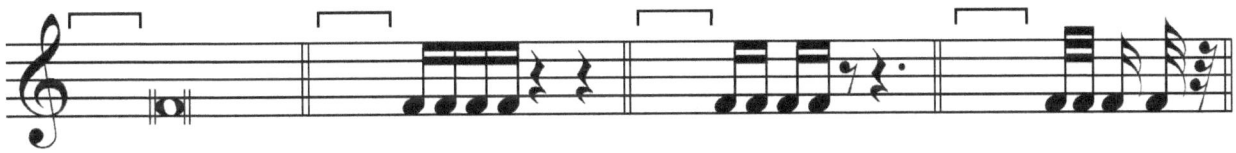

c) Add bar lines to complete the following rhythms.

5. a) Write the Melodic Interval below the given note. Use whole notes.

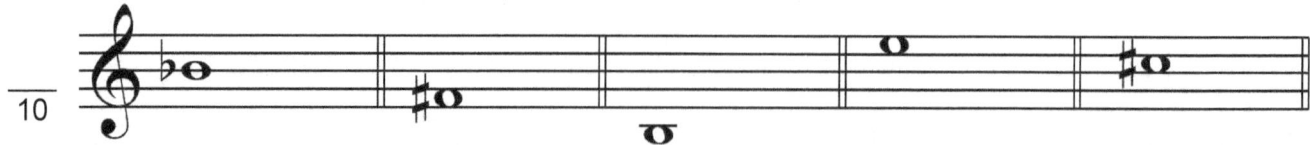

10

        Major 6   Augmented 2   minor 2   diminished 13   Perfect 12

    b) Write the Melodic Interval above the given note. Use whole notes.

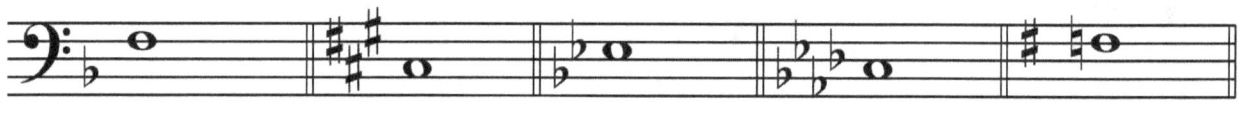

       Augmented 4   diminished 14   Perfect 8   Major 10   Augmented 1

    c) Name the following intervals.

___ ___ ___ ___ ___ ___ ___ ___ ___ ___

6. For each of the following Chords:
    a) Name the Chord Type as a Triad, Dominant Seventh or Quartal.
    b) Rewrite each Chord in the specified type of Open Score.

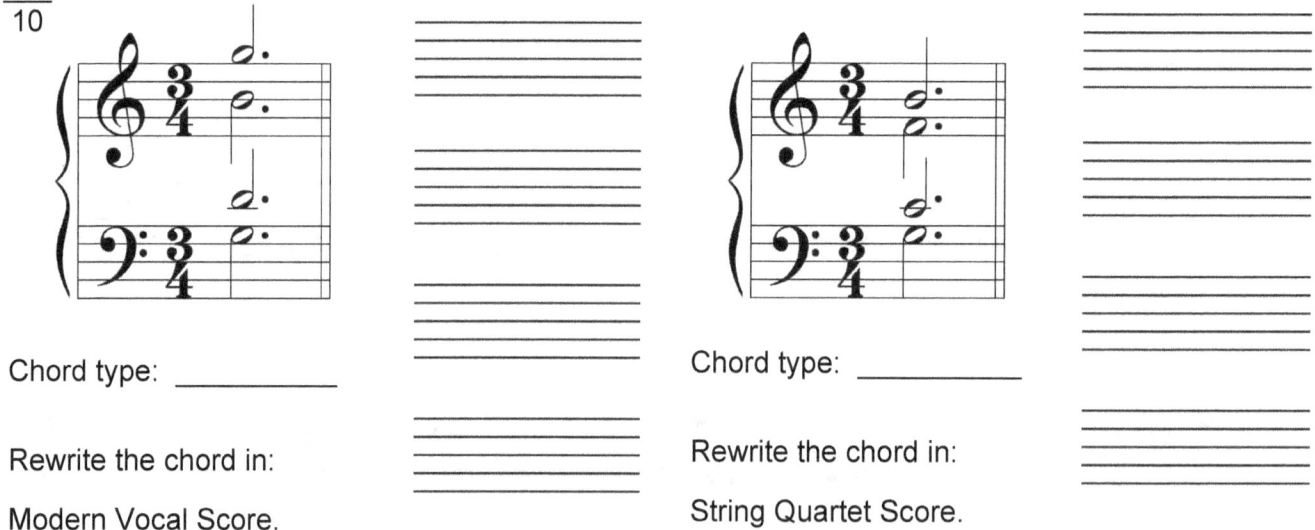

10

Chord type: _____

Chord type: _____

Rewrite the chord in:

Rewrite the chord in:

Modern Vocal Score.

String Quartet Score.

7. a) The following passage is written for Trumpet in B flat. Name the key in which it is written. Transpose it to Concert Pitch. Use the correct Key Signature. Name the new key.

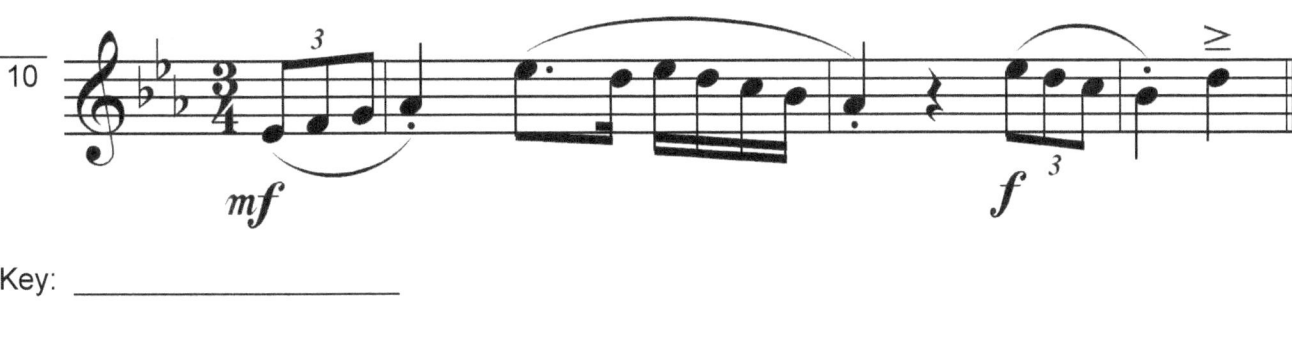

Key: _____

Key: _____

b) Name the Key of the following melody. Transpose it down into the key of f sharp minor using the correct Key Signature. Name the Interval of Transposition.

Key: _____

Interval of Transposition: _____

8.   a) For the following Melodic Opening:

    i)   Name the key of the melody.
    ii) Complete the given melodic opening to create a Question Phrase. End on an unstable
         scale degree. Name the Cadence. (There will be more than one correct answer.)
    iii) Compose an Answer Phrase to create a **Contrasting Period**. End on a stable scale
         degree. Name the Cadence. (There will be more than one correct answer.)
    iv) Draw a phrase mark (slur) over each phrase.

$\frac{}{10}$

Key: _____   Cadence: _____

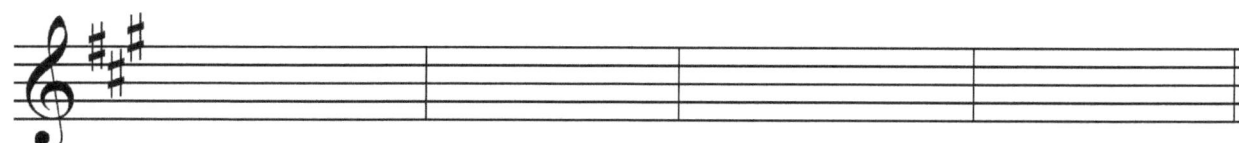

                                      Cadence: _____

    b) For each of the following melodies:

    i)   Name the key of the melody.
    ii) Write the Functional Chord Symbols on the lines below each measure.
    iii) Circle the non-chord tones and label each as **pt** or **nt**.

Key: _____

Key: _____

9. a) Provide the definition for FIVE (5) of the following terms.

10

   i) *sforzando*: _____

   ii) *con sordino*: _____

   iii) *l'istesso tempo*: _____

   iv) *comodo*: _____

   v) *volti subito*: _____

   vi) *sotto voce*: _____

   vii) *morendo*: _____

   viii) *martellato*: _____

   b) Choose the correct description to identify any FIVE (5) of the following statements.

   i) A source of melodic improvisation in Indian Classical Music:
   ☐ - Raga.   ☐ - Sitar.

   ii) An anonymous 13th century round:
   ☐ - El grillo.   .   ☐ - Sumer Is Icumen In.

   iii) A morality play by Hildegard von Bingen:
   ☐ - Ordo Virtutum.   ☐ - Gamelan Prawa.

   iv) A frottola by Josquin des Prez:
   ☐ - Evening Raga.   ☐ - El grillo.

   v) A single voice texture:
   ☐ - Homophonic.   ☐ - Monophonic.

   vi) A Javenese Ensemble consisting mainly of metallophones:
   ☐ - Gamelan.   ☐ - Sitar.

   vii) A recurring rhythmic or melodic pattern:
   ☐ - Ostinato.   ☐ - Plainchant.

   viii) A motion that occurs when two voices move in the opposite direction:
   ☐ - Oblique.   ☐ - Contrary.

10. Analyze the final excerpt from Ultimate Music Theory Student Olivia Allen's Sonatina in C Major by answering the questions below.

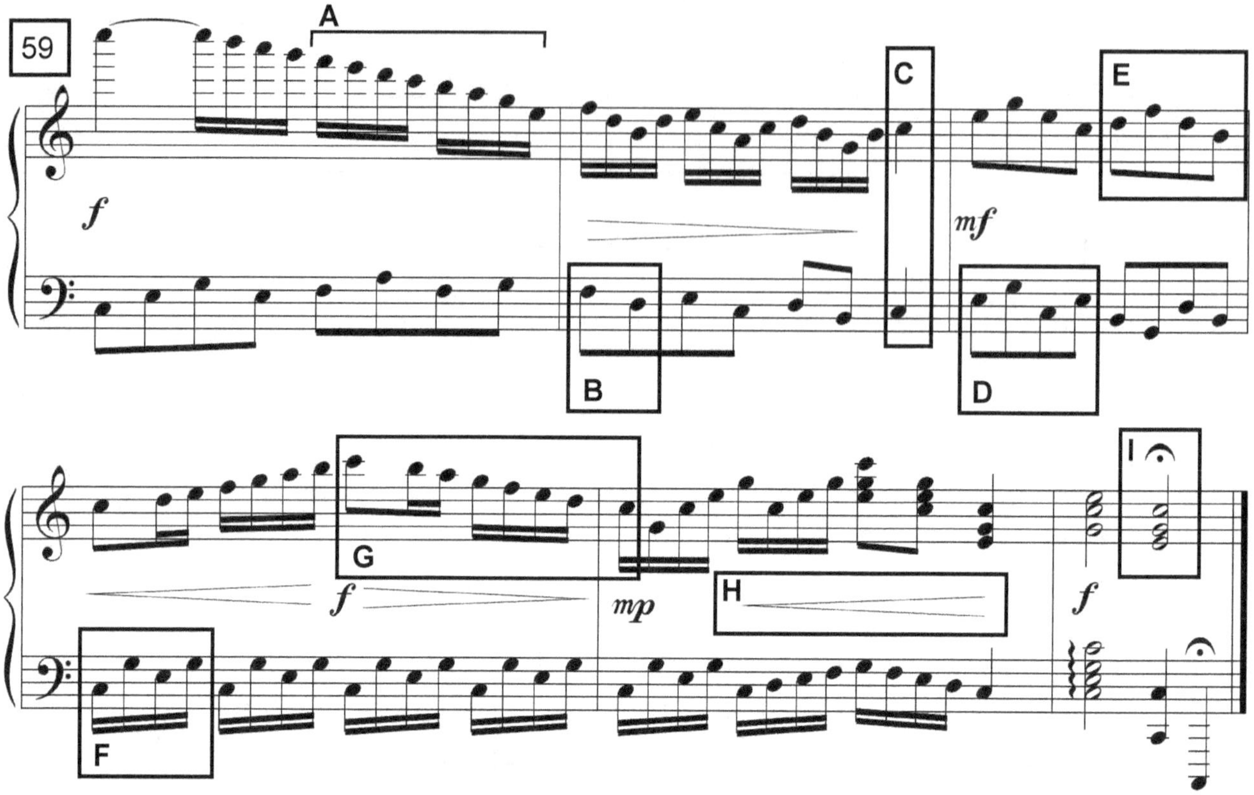

a) Identify the note names below **A**: _____, _____, _____, _____, _____, _____, _____, _____.

b) For the Interval at **B**, identify the type as: Melodic   or   Harmonic.

c) For the Interval at **C**, identify the type as: Simple   or   Compound.

d) Identify the interval at letter **B**. _____.   Identify the interval at letter **C**. _____.

e) For the Triad at **D**, identify: Root: _____   Quality: _____   Position: _____.

f) For the Triad at **E**, identify: Root: _____   Quality: _____   Position: _____.

g) Identify the number of times the Ostinato Pattern at **F** is played in Measure 62: _____ .

h) Identify the Scale at **G**: _____.   Identify the direction: _____.

i) Identify and Explain the sign at **H**: _____.

j) Identify and Explain the sign at **I**: _____.

TOP 10 Ultimate Music Theory Tips
To Score 100% on Exams

Tip #1: Students should complete at least 8 Practice Examinations before writing their Final Exam. LEVEL 8 Exams will have two hours to be completed.

Tip #2: Hold a "Practice Examination" in your studio. Have all students who are writing their Exams come at the same time. They can only bring a ruler, eraser and pencil. Set a Timer. When the timer starts, the examination begins – no talking, no cell phones, no open books!

Tip #3: Pizza Party! On the night before their Examinations, have a "Pizza Party" – Use the Ultimate Music Theory Flashcards App, UMT Whiteboard and UMT Games to review terminology and concepts. Everyone will have fun and everything will be fresh in their minds.

Tip #4: On Exam day, Students should arrive 15 minutes before the start time of their Examination.

Tip #5: If the Student is not given a piece of blank paper to use to write out their UMT Map before beginning their Examination, they should ask for one from the Exam Center Representative. (Have your Student practice asking for a blank piece of paper.)

Tip #6: Remind both Student and Parent that it is the Student's responsibility to bring a mechanical pencil (with extra lead), or 2 - 3 pencils (with a pencil sharpener), eraser and ruler. They cannot bring any items that have "music" on them, so they cannot bring their UMT Rulers.

Tip #7: It is always a good idea to bring a tissue or two, a bottle of water and a couple of hard candies if it is cold/allergy time. Be sure to get plenty of rest the day before the exam.

Tip #8: Complete the exam in order beginning with question 1. Review what your Student can do if they get stuck – if their brain goes blank on a question. One suggestion would be to continue to the next question and then go back later to finish that question.

Tip #9: Remind Students to look at the front AND back of each page to ensure that ALL questions have been answered… and checked… and double checked.

Tip #10: Ultimate Music Theory 100% Club - *The Way to Score Success!* You and your student can become a member of the UMT 100% Club when your student receives a score of 100% on their nationally recognized theory exams including the RCM Theory Examinations.

Go to UltimateMusicTheory.com and complete the UMT 100% Club Form to receive your special 100% Club Certificate & Congratulations!

 **Workbooks, Exams, Answers, Online Courses, App & More!**

A Proven Step-by-Step System to Learn Theory Faster - from Beginner to Advanced.

Innovative techniques designed to develop a complete understanding of music theory, to enhance sight reading, ear training, creativity, composition and musical expression.

All UMT Series have matching Answer Books!

The UMT Rudiments Series - Beginner A, Beginner B, Beginner C, Prep 1, Prep 2, Basic, Intermediate, Advanced & Complete (All-In-One)

♪ 12 Lessons, Review Tests, and a Final Exam to develop confidence
♪ Music Theory Guide & Chart for fast and easy reference of theory concepts
♪ 80 Flashcards for fun drills to dramatically increase retention & comprehension

Rudiments Exam Series - Preparatory, Basic, Intermediate & Advanced

♪ 8 Exams plus UMT Tips on How to Score 100% on Theory Exams

Each Rudiments Workbook correlates to a Supplemental Workbook.

The UMT Supplemental Series - Prep Level, Level 1, Level 2, Level 3, Level 4, Level 5, Level 6, Level 7, Level 8 & Complete (All-In-One) Level

♪ Form & Analysis and Music History - Composers, Eras & Musical Styles
♪ Melody Writing using ICE - Imagine, Compose & Explore
♪ 12 Lessons, Review Tests, Final Exam and 80 Flashcards for quick study

Supplemental Exam Series - Level 5, Level 6, Level 7 & Level 8

♪ 8 Exams to successfully prepare for nationally recognized Theory Exams

UMT Online Courses, Music Theory App & More

♪ UMT Certification Course, Teachers Membership & Elite Educator Program
♪ Ultimate Music Theory App correlates to the Rudiments Workbooks
♪ Free Resources - Teachers Guide, Music Theory Blogs, videos & downloads

Go To: **UltimateMusicTheory.com**